To Maggie —
   In memory of a friendship
   that was too short...

           Love,
           M.A.

listen to the warm

By ROD McKUEN

listen
to
the
warm

ROD McKUEN

RANDOM HOUSE NEW YORK

Eleventh Printing

Manufactured in the United States of America by the Kingsport Press, Inc., Kingsport, Tennessee. Designed by Carl Weiss.

Here He Comes Again, Buffalo Grass, Like a Child, Dandelion Days, Through European Windows, Do You Know Me, Maria?, The Beautiful Strangers, That Time of Loving, The Snow and *The Love Creature*, used by permission of Editions Chanson, Los Angeles, California.

A Kind of Loving, The Far West, Stanyan Street, Times Gone By, Thank You, Me and the Cat, Three, Methinks Thou Doth Protest Too Much, The Grand Opening Going Out of Business Sale and *Song Without Words*, used by permission of Stanyan Music Co., Hollywood, California.

The Ever Constant Sea, lines and/or adaptations of poems entitled *Pushing the Clouds Away, While Drifting, The Time of Noon, The Days of the Dancing* and *Gifts from the Sea* (from the Anro Production for Warner Bros. Records, "The Sea"), used by permission of Warm Music Co., Sherman Oaks, California.

I'll Say Goodbye (Je Partirai), reprinted by permission of Le Rideau Rouge, rights for United States and United Kingdom controlled by Asa Music Company; music by Gilbert Becaud, French lyrics by Louis Amade, English lyrics by Rod McKuen.

If you cry when we leave Paris
I'll buy you a teddy bear all soft and gold.

CONTENTS

A CAT NAMED SLOOPY

1 |

For a while
the only earth that Sloopy knew
              was in her sandbox.
Two rooms on Fifty-fifth Street
              were her domain.
Every night she'd sit in the window
among the avocado plants
waiting for me to come home
    (my arms full of canned liver and love).
We'd talk into the night then
                contented
but missing something.
She the earth she never knew
me the hills I ran
          while growing bent.

Sloopy should have been a cowboy's cat
with prairies to run
                    not linoleum
and real-live catnip mice.
No one to depend on but herself.

I never told her
      but in my mind
I was a midnight cowboy even then.
Riding my imaginary horse
down Forty-second Street,
going off with strangers
to live an hour-long cowboy's life,
          but always coming home to Sloopy,
      who loved me best.

2 |

A dozen summers
we lived against the world.
An island on an island.
She'd comfort me with purring
I'd fatten her with smiles.
We grew rich on trust
        needing not the beach or butterflies
I had a friend named Ben
Who painted buildings like Roualt men.
                        He went away.
My laughter tired Lillian
after a time
    she found a man who only smiled.
Only Sloopy stayed and stayed.

Winter.
Nineteen fifty-nine.
Old men walk their dogs.
Some are walked so often
that their feet leave
      little pink tracks
in the soft gray snow.

Women fur on fur
      elegant and easy
only slightly pure
hailing cabs to take them
    round the block and back.
Who is not a love seeker
when December comes?
Even children pray to Santa Claus.
I had my own love safe at home
and yet I stayed out all one night
      the next day too.

3 |

They must have thought me crazy
      screaming
          Sloopy
      Sloopy
as the snow came falling
down around me.

I was a madman
to have stayed away
     one minute more
than the appointed hour.
I'd like to think a golden cowboy
snatched her from the window sill,
         and safely saddlebagged
   she rode to Arizona.
She's stalking lizards
in the cactus now perhaps
      bitter but free.

I'm bitter too
and not a free man any more.

        Once was a time,
in New York's jungle in a tree,
before I went into the world
in search of other kinds of love
nobody owned me but a cat named Sloopy.

        Looking back
perhaps she's been
the only human thing
that ever gave back love to me.

listen
to
the
warm

1

ONE

This is the way it was
while I was waiting for your eyes
                              to find me.
I was drifting
        going no place.
Hypnotized by sunshine
                    maybe,
barking back at seals along the beach.
Skipping flat stones on the water,
but much too wise for sand castles.
My castles were across the sea
or still within my mind.

There were the beach bars
and the other beach people
sometimes little bedrooms were my beach,
            but I was drifting.

I must have thought the night could save me
as I went down into pillows
        looked up through dirty windows
    smiled back from broken mattresses
turned in Thunderbirds
        and kissed in elevators.

I cried too sometimes.
        For me.

I loved every face I thought looked pretty
and every kindred eye I caught in crowds.
        But I was drifting,
                before you.

TWO

Be gentle with me, new love.
Treat me tenderly.
I need the gentle touch,
the soft voice,
the candlelight after nine.

There've been so many who didn't understand

so give me all the love I see in your timid eyes
but give it gently.
                    Please.

THREE

You see how easily we fit together,
as if God's own hand had cradled only us
and this beach town's population were but two
and this wide bed but a child's cradle
with room enough left over for presents.

Tomorrow I'll buy you presents.
Pomegranates and breadsticks,
tickets round the room and back
and red red roses like everybody buys everybody.

Everybody's got a diamond ring
          and Sunday shoes.
Neckties and petticoats,
pistols and tennis balls.

What pleases you?
     I'd hock my watch to buy you Greece
  or sell my car to bring you rickshaws from Rangoon.

All they had down at the corner
        were poppies with some lemon leaves.
They'll have to do
        till I can bring home Union Square.

I found a twenty-dollar bill when I was ten.
I bought a cardboard circus and a fountain pen
and a jackknife because I never had one before.
My mother thought I'd stolen the money.
I brought her perfume from the dime store.
                    She believed me then.

I was rich in those days,
for a week I had everything.

I wish I'd known you then.

FOUR

What I know of friendly winds
I've learned from being on the sea
      sailing no place
going with the wind
making every harbor home.

I'll show you friendly places now
secret places known to only me.

      My toll beach where nobody goes
    A tree, *mon arbre.*
We may even see the wind together.

FIVE

You've been so long at the beach
you even taste like the sun
but the sun is much too warm
                         even for love.
I mean—I want you
but night is only inches away
                    and I can wait.
Meanwhile
watch the indolent butterfly playing on the tall flower
in the yard
and think about the sun's going down.
It always does you know.

SIX

You stand
among the awkward hollyhocks,
little breasts and big eyes,
love's machinery not yet working.
The dandelions trampled
the tall grass twisting in the wind
the lizard sulking in the sun.

You stand there
like some new flower
beautiful and ready to be picked.

This summer belongs
to the people of the world
who want each other.
The lonely have no right
                to share the summer sun.

SEVEN

We touch.
Shoulder-to-shoulder.
You can't do more when crossing streets
with mannequins in windows looking back.

I try to match your step—
that way I'm sure of staying close.
You smell like love.
That must be so
for what I smell is dear to me and *new*.

And so a little walk through town
becomes a journey
a love vacation from ourselves
but with ourselves.

Everything you say is funny
           or beautiful.

EIGHT

Clouds are not the cheeks of angels you know
they're only clouds.
                    Friendly sometimes,
but you can never be sure.
If I had longer arms
I'd push the clouds away
or make them hang above the water somewhere else,
but I'm just a man
                who needs and wants,
mostly things he'll never have.
Looking for that thing that's hardest to find—

I've been going a long time now
along the way I've learned some things.
            You have to make the good times yourself
take the little times and make them into big times
and save the times that are all right
            for the ones that aren't so good.

I've never been able
            to push the clouds away by myself.
                    Help me.

Please.

NINE

Dirty old men have the best lot after all.
                                    Courage.
    Ask a pretty girl her name,
nothing is the worst she'll say . . .

Follow women after dark
they can only yell for help or whisper *yes.*

I lie here dying of delight at being close
matching you in sleep breath for breath
                              yet awake.

     A coward
because I will not love you into waking.
Brave because I wait.
    You'll turn to me;
I hope I'm finally sleeping when you do
              (or both awake).
I wouldn't want my love to go unnoticed.

All those years I had to love my hands
    I must have been a madman.
I conquered film stars for my need
    but that was long before your shoulders.

listen to the warm

TEN

You might have been a nun in love with God
thinking men not good enough to see
                         your close-cropped hair
or know your midnight eyes.

A drum majorette perhaps, with batteried baton
who dreamed of Radio City on the football field.
Such a childhood might have led you to the silver screen
and not into my arms.

We might have gone through other gardens then
and never known this park.
I might have closed my eyes in age one day
never having seen you walk.
Never having heard you scold my unshaven chin
or open up your arms to let me in
                         unshaven but not afraid.

I'm grateful then for your upbringing—
it led you like an arrow here
uncomplicated and mine.

ELEVEN

The afternoon shadows
gather as the day goes home.
And now the in-between time
            before the night
        after the day.

Above the gray harbor
the city sits on white houses
waiting for the happenings
and all the boats are in.

A wind is coming up
and we'll be warmer by ourselves at home.
        I cannot look at you
reflected in the glass behind this bar
                much longer.

I want to be alone with you,
I want my thighs to speak your name
so softly only you can hear.

This place was made
for those who still play hide-and-seek
            we're home free.

TWELVE

See the dog
      he doesn't move—a voyeur.
             Never mind.
What we've done is beautiful.
For gods and animals to see,
for us to stand aside in awe
    and look ourselves up and down.

Your breasts are just your breasts, that's all,
          but letting go to me
    detaching from me all the debts I've paid that day—
       smiles to secretaries mean
          dividends to competition in my work,
          courtesy to those who'd break me down,
          good morning to the elevator man.

Your thighs make over all the scales
and so I hurry home to you
to use your belly as a cape
            to cover up the day.

THIRTEEN

Listen
I don't apologize for being hard to know
                    I am what I am
sulking will not change that
but apple pies and warm hands help
and I have never known a cat
that couldn't calm me down
by walking slowly past my chair.

So I'll smile for you in winter
if you'll go easy
and fill your rooms with roses when I can
if you'll stop beating me with words
and if in bed
you never turn away . . .

2

FOURTEEN

How can we be sure of anything
           the tide changes.
The wind that made the grain wave gently yesterday
       blows down the trees tomorrow.
And the sea sends sailors crashing on the rocks,
as easily as it guides them safely home.
         I love the sea
but it doesn't make me less afraid of it
         I love you
but I'm not always sure of what you are
and how you feel.

I'd like to crawl behind your eyes
and see me the way you do
        or climb through your mouth
and sit on every word that comes up through your throat.

Maybe I could be sure then
                    maybe I could know
as it is—I hide beneath your frowns
or worry when you laugh too loud.
                    Always sure a storm is rising.

FIFTEEN

I have loved you
in so many ways
in crowds or all alone.
When you were sleeping beside me.
When you were away
and I imagined others watching you in the street
or worse—you in other people's arms.

I have seen the march of beach birds and loved you.
I have lent myself to summer sun and loved you.
And seeing naked trees
              and raising my collar to the wind
and counting minutes till chartered hours were there
I have loved you.

And the questions never asked.
The answers learned at love's expense.
I've promised myself.
I will not ask where you have been tonight
I'll only say hello
              and hope.

SIXTEEN

I know a tree beyond the bend ahead
that drags its branches in the water
beneath it there is yellow grass
    and colored stones.
If you can shake your new friend from your mind
we'll go down along the water's edge
    and give ourselves another chance.

Think about the squirrels darting in the fallen leaves
    consider the changing clouds.
The crickets are still singing in the grass
think of how they'll sound when Christmas comes again.

This is daylight.
Turn and face me face-to-face.
We'll go naked in the afternoon
and then you'll see I'm only me.
Were you expecting something more?

I taste like you—remember
because I've been with you so long
because we are each other as we are ourselves.
All I have to fight
is what I've been for you before.

SEVENTEEN

As leaves blow along the beach
and the bleached starfish are washed upon the shore
             I wait
           anticipating nothing.
Not pretending anymore or daring to imagine
uncertain even of spring, I wait.

Sometimes I put a sea shell to my ear
and it all comes back,
      the children
             that day
the kildear birds marching in formation
down to the sea and back
      down to the sea and back.
Even the gypsies.

EIGHTEEN

I stood watching
as you crossed the street
            for the last time.
Trying hard to memorize you.
Knowing it would be important.
The way you walked,
the way you looked back over your shoulder at me.

Years later
I would hear the singing of the wind
and that day's singing would come back.
That time of going would return to me
every sun-gray day.
April or August it would be the same
            for years to come.

Man has not made the kind of bromide
that would let me sleep without your memory
or written erotically enough
to erase the excitement of just your hands.

These long years later it is worse
for I remember what it was
as well as what it might have been.

32   *listen to the warm*

3

NINETEEN

Midsummer
is not the only reason I am going home
        to the yellow corn
and the grasshopper playing in the tall grass
and the indolent butterfly darting from marigold to rose
and back again.

I am going home again to meet the dreaded winter
                and the unsure spring.
And the girl whose eyes never left mine
when we swam together in the river
                and made love
below the old brick bridge.

I am going home
to see if there really is such a place as home.

It takes a long time
        for a single blossom to fall
    from a flower tree.
And I have so much time to spare
that I can watch all the flowers fall
            from all the trees.

TWENTY

People riding trains are nice
they offer magazines
and chocolate-covered cherries,
the details you want most to know
                  about their recent operations.
If I'd been riding home to you
I could have listened with both ears
but I was on my way away.

Across from me
there was a girl crying
                (long, silent tears)
while an old man held her hand.
It was only a while ago you said,
Take the seat by the window,
                you'll see more.

I filled the seat beside me
with my coat and books.
I'm antisocial without you.
I'm antiworld and people too.

Sometimes I think
I'll never ride a train again.
At least not away.

TWENTY-ONE

Only a day away
the loneliness is unbearable.
How will it be if you are a year gone?

What will happen
if I am not to know again
                your warm arms
your shoulder next to my face at night
the quiet talk over strong coffee
the chase along the toll beach
                    and oh God
so many things.

I am afraid of being alone now
it happens every time you close the door
or go into the next room
             away from me.

I am like a child again
I can't be left alone.

Hurry.

TWENTY-TWO

Moments ago
the ducks played on the millpond
and the sparrows chatted freely
and the chickens poked and pecked
                        about the yard.

Then with the first shadow of evening
                        they were all gone.
Last to go the kildear birds
off beyond the eucalyptus trees.

Standing at the window I often wonder
why the kildear birds
        are always last to leave.

TWENTY-THREE

On this Tuesday away from you
I wonder if the time will ever pass
till we're together
even for a while again.

But yesterday you touched me
and we drove to the toll beach
and ran in the sand.
Sorry no one could see
how beautifully happy we were.

TWENTY-FOUR

What I can see beyond this wall
is greenness nothing more.
Not children or a house
only trees and greenness.

And as I walk about the yard
        content with only green
I hear the sound of summer coming once again
in the sky and on the hills.

It's summer in the city too
you're dancing with yourself
and sleeping with your pillow.
So I tell myself.

My microscopic eye
can see beyond this wall.
But there's another wall beyond.

TWENTY-FIVE

Where were we
when the coming of the rain
made us turn from conversation to the window?

In mustard fields maybe,
            or the love jungle,
and as we talked
we were with others, not ourselves.

I was thinking of old birthdays and holidays gone wrong
                and pretty people seen on streetcars
        but never met.
Selling soda bottles to pay for movie matinées.
        I was twelve.
        Tarzan was the man I most resembled in those days.
How can I have grown so old without once swinging on a
        vine?
            Did you think of party dresses
        and high school plays
                or hallways full of lovers not yet met?

The mind is such a junkyard;
                it remembers candy bars
                        but not the Gettysburg Address,
        Frank Sinatra's middle name
                but not the day your best friend died.

If in your mind there is some corner
        not yet occupied with numbers you may never need,
remind your memory of the day
            we turned to watch the rain
    and turning back forgot
        that we belonged to one another.

TWENTY-SIX

Leaves fall down now
      brown and beautiful
   brittle to the touch
lying on the ground or filling public fountains.
Swirling down the street,
catching in the gutters
         and diverting little streams of water.

Brown October leaves
      trampled under foot
banged about by brooms that sweep the gutters clean.

I remembered today
that among the silly things you saved
         was a brown and yellow leaf
pressed between the pages of a book somewhere.

We found it in the park, remember?

I shook out every book I owned to find it.
                  Still it's lost,
or owned these days by Hemingway or Whitman.
Maybe even Gertrude Stein.
My God would she know what to do
               with a brown and yellow leaf?
And would she give it back?

TWENTY-SEVEN

The fireflies gone now
the trees low bending
with the weight of winter rain
I listen for the sound of winters past.
The years I walked the rainy streets
and filtered through the parks
in search of music people.
Creeping home to bed alone
to be with imaginary lovers
and hear the sound of Eden
ringing in my young ears.

I could go back to San Francisco
if I still had muscled thighs.
The trouble is
      I run a little faster now.

TWENTY-EIGHT

You won't believe this
but I'm going off to war
I know that's hard to understand.
To think of me knee-deep in mud
when I so love the sand.

When I so love the water
to run along the beach and play
it's hard to think of killing someone
on a beach someday.

That's what they want of me, you know
that's what I'm training for.
To think I used to think our fights
were tantamount to war.

TWENTY-NINE

Sitting on the hill today
I watched the fog
making its way past rooftops
and down along the trees
till it was by my side
and all about me.

Even the river on the land below was gone
as brown October opened up her arms and let the mist go
    free.
Coming up the hill a never-ending column of uniformed
    men.

I never thought I'd fall in love with you either
or send you long misspelled letters
that came back to me unopened.
I didn't need this time.

And now the mist from on the mountains
comes along the town
gathers as the darkness shrouds the world,
hides the lone dog smelling at the pavement
the wretched beggars
the street urchins sleeping in the railway station
and the women in dirty aprons shining shoes.

Against the sky
a farmer leads his cattle home.
A soldier
thumbs a ride from a passing jeep
as the beer hall
with its peeling walls and overhead steam pipes
and dark corners smelling of urine
closes for the night.

THIRTY

Snowfall in wild and dizzy patterns
                      quiet
      saddened snowfall.
It's quiet snow that I remember best.
Snowfall and Brahms
on November nights at Columbia.

You were inattentive
busying yourself with woman's work
and I would lie upon the bed
picking out imperfections in the ceiling
        till you were ready for me.

THIRTY-ONE

For a long time
after she closed the door behind her
and her footsteps ceased echoing down the hall,
I lay on the bed listening to the Soba man
playing his sad horn outside the window.

It's the same Tokyo spring
I knew a year ago.
Fewer strangers walk the dark streets now
and those who do have solitary ways.
They go along their private rivers
to their private beds
and I to mine—alone
never needing the comradeship of strangers more.

THIRTY-TWO

First aid.
Last rites.
The hour-to-hour way we live.
God is in our minds every time we hit the trench
an hour later true-time takes over
and fills us up with love remembered
or good-time love to come.

I killed a man today.
The only thing I'd hurt before
was you one time while making love
and then I only kissed too hard.

How does it feel to kill?
Like dying lonesome and unloved yourself.
Like cutting living grass,
or loosing all your marbles
in a match that wasn't right.

They are not dummies
on an infiltration field
the silent enemy breathes too.
Someone should have told me that
before I ran that endless field.

When true-time takes me over now
after God has held my mind awhile,
            I think of love.
I love my fellow man
      perhaps a little more today.
Tomorrow I'll go gently then
and give the other side a chance.

THIRTY-THREE

While I stood watch last night
you walked in sunlight
         another world away.

Afterward, down the alley from the PMO
I slept warm in closer arms
         and smelled the wood smoke.

Driving back along the KMAG road this morning
I saw soldiers walking hand-in-hand.
An old woman carried a paper umbrella
         and a baby on her back.
Near the compound gate a girl laughed.

All day I waited for the sun to come.
All day I listened for the rain to stop.
         Now as evening starts
    only the lowing of the cattle
breaks the monotone of rain.

THIRTY-FOUR

The bronze-bellied men of war
lie upon their narrow cots
and search the ceiling.
Oblivious to the wall of night.

Eternity sneaks in
her arms full of wild promises.
The young men go to sleep
to dream of Technicolor battles.

Yesterday the world was singing.
Hell was miles away.

But after a while the singing stops.

THIRTY-FIVE

One day I'll follow the birds
disappearing into the rain

                    going in a hurry,
                        then gone.

Glad to be in flight again
but not sure why I'm running.

There are some wounds I never
               speak about.
Some things that words have done to me
that none will ever know.

But one gray day
I'll follow a funeral out of town
        on the heels of the birds
               disappearing into the rain.

THIRTY-SIX

I live alone.
It hasn't always been that way.
It's nice sometimes
        to open up the heart a little
and let some hurt come in.
It proves you're still alive.

I'm not sure what it means.
Why we cannot shake the old loves from our minds.
It must be that we build on memory
and make them more than what they were.
        And is the manufacture
just a safe device for closing up the wall?

I do remember.
The only fuzzy circumstance
is sometimes where-and-how.
Why, I know.

It happens just because we need
to want and to be wanted too,
when love is here or gone
to lie down in the darkness
                and listen to the warm.

**the
grand
opening
going-
out-of-
business
sale**

THE DAYS OF THE DANCING

When I think of love
I think of Line's room where everything begins and ends,
of songs like *Lilac Wine* and *When the World Was
    Young,*
of girls I knew beneath the chinaberry tree at home
                                    when I was younger.

Walking after midnight expecting something.
The women in the Silver Dollar Bar in San Francisco
rubbing up against the sailors home on leave.
            Hearing Beretta sing sad songs at the Jackpot.
A girl fanning herself
under a forty-watt bulb in a room in Teague
offering me and my buddy a *package job.*

Is love collective?
Not any more it's not.
We're lucky if it lives above the jukebox bleat.

And so when I think of love and loving
I think of people dying alone for lack of love.
The skeletons of kites
        setting off treetops and telephone lines.
Wild strawberry blossoms that decorate hills otherwise
    green.
The solitary things.
For it is not the normal thing *to love*
in these times.
            It goes against the grain.
It is one plane the psychedelic mind has closed.

These are the days of the dancing—six feet apart.
The discothèque has tapped that time of loving into time.

Mr. Roebuck still likes Mr. Sears.
Abercrombie's stuck with Fitch all these years.
There must be others out there somewhere.

the grand opening going-out-of-business sale   59

When I think of love,
            and I do all the time,
I call up Flo and she says *come on over*
and we'll drive down to Trancas at the beach.
                        It's something to do.
It is at that.
Better than reading *Alice in Wonderland*
        now called *Valley of the Dolls.*
Wonderland is still there waiting, Alice,
it didn't die with Marilyn or Kennedy
(though the Rolling Stones have killed it once or twice)
it's living somewhere in the sticks.

We're only killing off the need.

Remember the athletes' mouths
they used to paint around the hole on Broadway
that puffed out Camel smoke?
                     That was love.
Graffiti on a billboard wall MAKE DATE—I LUV YOU.
In the end I suppose the athletes were not paid enough
to let their mouths be stretched that far.
But oh some tourists went home happy in those days
                     full of smoky dreams.

The magazines are filled with foreign bodies now.
They are not love.
We can't identify with them.
When I think of love I think about the corner bar.
                It was always good to me.
But even it's gone topless now.

God let us be different.
Let's not wear mustaches and funny clothes.
Let's not let our hair grow so long
it covers up our eyes
            and makes us unable to see the world.
Never mind the world—let's not miss each other.

They can keep their butterfly collections
their nineteen-thirties songs and one-room trips.
I want to see the world within the circle of your arms
and sail the wide sea of your thighs.

These are the days of the dancing
                  six feet apart.
And what was your first name anyway?

ON BORROWING

A man is killed in Hindustan
        I feel the bullet in my head.
A child is crying in the street
her tears could be my own.
I know that animals help man
when slaughtered on the doctor's couch
but dead dogs by the roadside
stay with me for days.

I find it hard to understand why someone takes my words
        from me.
        A friend?
Once upon a time he was
but then he stole my sea
        and my zodiacs as well.
            Ideas are few
another might not come by soon.

I had a pet raccoon
        who took my toothbrush once
but only to another room.

for Michael Strater

ROW THE BOAT ASHORE

My friend Michael wants to be a poet
he has the right credentials.
Once a phallic cymbol player
        in a burlesque band
he kept his eye upon the navel
not upon the orange.
Hard to do when you love bodies,
barfly or barbell types.

Michael's words ring right.
He's learned there is a world of *grays*
even in the dead of night.

Still he reads Ann Landers' vice to the lovelorn
    but skirts the prayboy philosophy.
 He prays for ideal love instead.
Rightly so.
He wants to be a poet.

for Lalo

HERE HE COMES AGAIN

Here he comes again, head high and smiling
shakin' down the world, playin' it cool.
He smiles as though he never been
hunted by the crowd, beaten by all the fools.

Think of all the men who never knew the answers
think of all of those who never even cared.
Still there are some who ask why
who want to know, who dare to try.
Every now and then we meet that kind of man
here he comes again and now he's gone.

for Jesse Pearson

THE TIME OF NOON

When you're alone at night
and the old memories you call back
to help you do the things
that will put you to sleep
don't work any more
and even the aphrodisiac of magazines
                                doesn't help
and there is no place to go, no one to call,
try thinking about the sun.

The way it catches in the trees sometimes.
The way it follows you while riding in a car.
The way it plays in the hair of strangers on the beach.
The way it climbs hills with you and pushes you from bed
                                in morning.

Think about the time of noon
when everybody's just a little crazy.

Remember that the cliffs are white and steep
and you'll grow tired climbing them
                        tired enough to sleep.

What you're thinking about
isn't really the cause of perspiration on your forehead
                        it's only the sun.
It's just the time of noon.

JULIE

If her mother's womb had had a view
she never would have ventured out.
As it is she travels subways
and sleeps in cellars
and wears a Garbo hat against the sun.

Fluorescent mirrors in public johns
were meant to kill our good conceptions of ourselves.
Haunting jade eyes turn apple-green
the rosy mouth becomes an ultraviolet pouch
and pores the craters of the moon.
And so she went away to live in Venice
                    wearing no make-up
        loving candlelight
and envying Cinderella.
Mama Cass is beautiful
but someone should have told poor Julie
        the Beats have all gone home.
My God, they've even closed the Big Sur Baths!

NO

Mini-skirts and pop-art ties
are more than modern man can bear.
The next thing Bloomingdale's will sell
is silver-coated underwear
or maybe cotton-candy wigs
edible for those who like
tattoos on their flabby pecks
foxtails on their motorbikes.

Yes I like the sound of rain
though not caught in a Dixie cup
and I must confess a thrill
on hearing bathtubs filling up.
There is a fetish for us all
each of us has his own twitch.
I'll take a benny now and then
but sugar cubes are far too rich.

DOUG DAVIS, THREE

While you were dying
I was going to the beach.
Unaware your smile
had caught fire at Orly
ten thousand miles away.

It was days later I learned
that you had walked your last deserted street,
crossed the line of infinity you had always tried to paint.

No longer smiling.
No more to run and chase the dappled dragonfly.

I would rather you had died breathing sea
                                 instead of smoke.
I lost your smile going down the stairs.

FOLK SONG FOR JUDY

I gave my love a cherry
and she spit the seed at me.
I gave my love a chicken
and she choked on the bones.
I gave my love a baby
        and she went away.

My analyst has cured me
of my self-destruction tendencies
but he's made of me instead a voyeur.
Every evening while waiting
to be ushered from his waiting room,
I go to the window
        and watch the people
    in the apartment house across the way
going to the bathroom.

I never see my doctor any more
I know that's very mean
I thought he was a friend of mine.
He thought I was James Dean.

for Herb Alpert

THE DANCE

The strong young bulls
don't come to the ring
      to die on Sunday.
They come to show a man their energy
                their pride.
The dancing that they've practiced all their lives
to bring to the arena one August afternoon.

Their partners are not killers then.
They're dancers too.
     Their red capes flashing.
Three-cornered hats that scoop applause
           when the dancing's done.

Pity not the strong young bull.
        He takes his chance.
    As does the matador.
The price for coming to the dance.

Young men pretty in the sun
against the handsome bulls.
           Killers?   No.
Only dancers in the dance.
To see the dancing is to know.

I don't believe that really
     I'm of the Taurus sign
and every dead bull in the ring is my relation.

for Gordon

FIRST AND LAST VISIT
TO AN ANNEX IN BURBANK

Time was you couldn't see the Forest Lawn
                for the trees.
Not so any more.
Real estate is real estate and lumber's only lumber,
it used to make a fine pine box.
(They don't make caskets out of pine these days
                they're made of bent John Birch.)
But the graveyard's open every night for your inconvenience
and plastic trees at Christmas time fill every loved one's
        need.

On hearing The Wedgie Shoe King had died
I went to pray at empty shrines
While I was there there came a scraping
        not unlike the sound of slugs
that slide along the sidewalks aiming for the lawn.
Imagination?

                        No.
Only the friendly dead calling HELP.

FADE IN, PHASE OUT

Busby Berkley must be smiling now
        to see so many hoofers
dancing up and down the White House steps.
The Late Show's like the Senate
where all the corridors ring out
        the sound of Muzak.

Listen I won't vote again
till Rocky runs for President
        (not Nelson, Hudson)
and Mae West runs for Vice.

As for Foreign Affairs
        they interest me.
    I've had a few.

If only Mr. Fields were here
               he'd have a time.
There are no children any more
except for Shirley Temple Black and Orphan Annie
(at least the second of the two likes dogs).
I don't know where they went.
In search of psychedelic kumquats maybe.
They're not behind the barnyard smoking cigarettes.
               Or at the barber shop.

THE GRAND OPENING
GOING-OUT-OF-BUSINESS SALE

Mad dogs rumble in the jungle come and see it for a penny.
Where is hope there isn't any. Set your course and sail
for the grand opening going-out-of-business sale.

Truth like buffalo is dying. Can you spare a dollar buddy?
Streets and stars alike are muddy. Shop and save by mail
at the grand opening going-out-of-business sale.

The moon is so monotonous I guess it's lost its pull.
Lady you can't stay here long the parking lot is full.

All the new and fancy dances now are done a mile apart.
Don't you dare to steal my heart unless you've got the bail
at the grand opening going-out-of-business sale.

**twenty-
two
songs**

THE WORLD I USED TO KNOW

Someday some old familiar rain
will come along and know my name.
And then my shelter will be gone
and I'll have to move along.
But till I do I'll stay awhile
and track the hidden country of your smile.

Someday the man I used to be
will come along and call on me.
And then because I'm just a man
you'll find my feet are made of sand.
But till that time I'll tell you lies
and chart the hidden boundaries of your eyes.

Someday the world I used to know
will come along and bid me go.
Then I'll be leavin' you behind
for love is just a state of mind.
But till that day I'll be your man
and love away your troubles if I can.

for Sloopy and Batman

ME AND THE CAT

We've seen so many winters come
and watched so many old years go
and held so many hands at dawn
we never really got to know.
Lying down someplace shady and flat,
me in my shirttails, him with his whiskers
                    me and the cat.

We've done so many foolish things
and yet the days have served us well.
We've given all our smiles away
when there were some we cared to sell.
Livin' the good life without gettin' fat,
me in my shirttails, him with his whiskers
                    me and the cat.

Looking back few friends had we
but I've got him and he's got me.

And when the golden minute comes
when we no longer wake to smell
the river where the wild swans sailed
the orchard where the blossoms fell,
we'll smile a little thinkin' of that.
Me in my shirttails, him with his whiskers
                    me and the cat.

for Jerry Moss

THE LOVERS

Up from the pastures of boredom
out from the sea of discontent
they come in packs like hungry hounds
the seekers of the dark enchantment.

They haunt the boulevards and bars
they pray to wishing wells and stars
they ride the hurricane of hope
not looking back but on they go.
Toward the distance and deceiving
and all the while they keep believing
that they are special and apart.
The lovers. The lovers of the heart.
     The lovers.

And when they pair off two-by-two
they feel they are the chosen few
because their beds are made of straw
that feels like velvet in the night.
And so the night is never-ending
it's made of distance and pretending
that they are special and apart.
The lovers. The lovers of the heart.
                                    The lovers.

And when love goes away, and when love goes
good-bye catches in their throats like cotton.
Rises in their hearts like rain.
The good times suddenly are all forgotten.
The hunt begins again.

They search the subways and the street
their faces tired like their feet
their bodies aching to be warm
and so they hide behind the moon.
Their loneliness inside them growing
but they take comfort in just knowing
that they are special and apart.
The lovers. The lovers of the heart.
                    The lovers.

And when love comes again, and when love comes
hello rises from their throats like singing.
Catches in their hearts like wind.
The good things strangers in their arms are bringing
makes life all right again.

They turn their faces to the light
no longer hiding in the night
so unashamed and unafraid
that they can face each other's faults.
And though the waltz will have its ending
there's no harm in just pretending
that they are special and apart.
The lovers. The lovers of the heart.
                    The lovers.

SONG WITHOUT WORDS

I wanted to write you some words you'd remember
words so alert they'd leap from the paper
and crawl up your shoulder and lie by your ears
and be there to comfort you down through the years.
But it was cloudy that day and I was lazy
and so I stayed in bed just thinking about it.

I wanted to write you and tell you that maybe
love songs from lovers are unnecessary.
We are what we feel and writing it down
seems foolish sometimes without vocal sound.
But I spent the day drinking coffee, smoking cigarettes
and looking in the mirror practicing my smile.

I wanted to write you one last, long love song
that said what I feel one final time.
Not comparing your eyes and mouth to the stars
but telling you only how like yourself you are.
But by the time I thought of it, found a pen,
put the pen to ink, the ink to paper,
you were gone.

And so, this song has no words.

THE FAR WEST
(Le Plat Pays)

And now the tumbleweed is rolling down the plain,
chased down the dunes by dust that's never known a rain.
It runs as frightened as a rabbit to its distant lair.
Down the diamond desert only God knows where.
Above the hills the clouds wait silently
as if they knew some secret not yet part of me
in the far west, my home.

And as the afternoon gives up the summer sun,
the shadows lengthen slowly one by one.
A million colors dart and dance and die across the sky.
An eager evening bids the dying day good-bye.
A man could live alone and never think it wrong
if the November wind didn't sing such lonesome songs
in the far west, my home.

And now the rain begins and as it starts to fall,
a silence like the breath of God comes down and covers all.
It's the last day of the year. No more fences left to clear.
Not another hill to climb. There just isn't any time.
With cold December just a frown away,
the tall trees lift their weary arms to pray
in the far west, my home.

I always thought that I'd die in my own bed.
Surrounded by the memories of the life I'd led.
Not mourned by many, but by just a chosen few.
The few who understood the things I tried so hard to do.
Now I'm dying all alone.
            Now I'm dying all alone.
                        Now I'm dying all alone.
With the November wind singing
in the far west, my home.

BUFFALO GRASS

Come, we'll all plant buffalo grass
and wade down ditches to the river
and each of us will take a lover,
someone new who'll never ask
why our eyes are puffed and red,
why our hopes of love are dead,
why we each go home to bed,
alone though we're together,
but never letting on
just growing older in the dawn
till the harvest finds us
no longer equal to the task
and cuts us down like so much buffalo grass.

THAT TIME OF LOVING

That time of loving may not come again
and so I've saved the old loves one by one
to call back when the leaves fall down
and winter covers all the town
and now is next to nothing
compared to where I've been.

That time of loving may not come again
or if it does it might not be the same
the loves remembered, those that last
have caught me living in the past
for now is next to nothing
compared to where I've been
and that time of loving may not come again.

LIKE A CHILD

Like a child I just sat in the sunlight
and played with the minutes as they went running by.
Like a child who had never known sorrow
I didn't hurry tomorrow I just looked at the sky.
While the clouds went on endlessly passing.
All the clouds on their long voyage home
seemed to say that youth is everlasting
but a rose cannot grow alone.

Like a child I would listen in silence
to the soft sound of evening as it caught up the day,
till you were there in the gathering darkness
and we found that our green years had all gone away.
Now the clouds are going forever
here awhile then gone evermore
and a child on the far side of never
has to run when time closes the door.

Then take my hand and as children we'll go now
all alone through the thundering crowds.
Take my hand and together we'll look now
like a child for the little lost clouds.

STANYAN STREET

There are golden apples to be picked
and green hills to climb
and meadows to run when you're young.

There are roaring rivers to be crossed
and bridges to build
and wild oats to sow as you grow.

But later on the other side of time
the apples no longer taste sweet.
Bridges fall down. Meadows turn brown
as life falls apart
in a little room on Stanyan Street.

listen to the warm

THROUGH EUROPEAN WINDOWS

1

You might have seen me down in Greece
harvesting October wheat
or along the rocky coast of Hydra.
Living like the sailors do
port to port, drink to drink.
Seeking friends and not so much a lover.
Through European windows you might have seen me.

Oh how it was when the boats came in.
The women went wild to welcome them in.
The children built fires tall and bright.
You could read through a man's soul by the light.
The blackness of evil looked whiter than white.
It's lucky we had such things to fill up the night.

I was a young man then and played at young men's games.
You should have seen me then, that time won't come again.

2

You might have seen me down in Spain.
Running down the Spanish plains
or beside the seas of Barcelona.
Living like the seagulls do,
Summer to summer, dune to dune.
Watching as the tide went rolling over.
Through European windows you might have seen me.

Down in the park where the sun shines Sunday
and no wind rattles the trees till Monday.
Where statues stand alone and forlorn
in memory of generals forgotten and gone.
A riderless horse trots home in the dawn.
It's lucky yesterday's hero fell on the lawn.

I was a soldier then and played at soldier games.
You should have seen me then, the general knew my name.

3

You might have seen me down in France
fourteenth of July in the dance
or along the hills of the Camargue.
Living like the cowboys do
roundup to roundup, smile to smile.
Riding herd then lying in the clover.
Through European windows you might have seen me.

Oh how it was to be driving all day
through the mud of December and the dust of May.
With the smell of the cattle and the taste of the rain
and the sound of the scythe as it tore through the grain
and the feel of your horse moving under your groin.
To sweat in summer and freeze when winter came.

I was a cowboy then, playing cowboy games.
You should have seen me then, riding down the plain.

4

You might have seen me anywhere.
Name a country, I was there.
Wasting time and only growing older.
Living like the nomads do
day-to-day but each day through.
Now the days are gone, the time is over.
Through European windows you might have seen me.

I was a cowboy then.
Through European windows you might have seen me.

TIMES GONE BY

Remember how we spent the nighttime counting out the
    stars.
Too late for the beach, too early for the bars.
All of us together would raise our glasses high
and drink a toast to times gone by.

The times, oh we had some times
when the world was the color of neon signs.
Each of us and all of us killed our dreams with rye
and tried to crowd a lifetime into times gone by.

Remember how the Sunday morning bells were always
    ringing
and out along the waterfront we'd hear the big men
    singing.
In some long-forgotten time, some August or July.
Even then we'd talk about the times gone by.

The times, oh we had some times
when love cost only nickels and dimes.
Always when our secret needs were hard to satisfy
we'd talk of going back again to times gone by.

Remember how we talked and laughed and cried into the
    dawning
and the terrible taste of kisses in the morning.
Crowded rooms and lonesome tunes and very little sky.
Even then the better times were times gone by.

The times, you know we had some times
with gentle women and vintage wines.
But that was when we didn't know our youth was passing
    by.
Now all we have to think about are times gone by.

THE SNOW

The snow, the snow keeps on falling
all white like the down of the dove.
The snow, the snow keeps on falling
worthless, like the tears you cry over love.

The lovers promenade like so many sheep
then home they go to the fire's glow
to smile and love and sleep.

And all the snowmen are melting away
the children go again on their way
while the snow, the snow keeps on falling
all white like the down of a dove.
The snow, the snow keeps on falling
worthless, like the tears you cry over love.

THE BEAUTIFUL STRANGERS

Ah the beautiful strangers
who held me for a night
and fell down in the darkness
on pillows soft and white.

Ah the beautiful strangers
all in the afternoon
who praised my flat little stomach
and came back to my room.

Ah the beautiful strangers
who spoiled me for a time
and taught me neon's just as nice
as afternoon sunshine.

for Mike Gould

I'LL SAY
GOOD-BYE

Now that the summer's come and gone I'll say good-bye.
Now that the winter's comin' on I'll say good-bye.
I'm not the first man or the last
who had a thirst to leave the past.
So while the autumn rain is falling I'll say good-bye.

For every star that falls to earth a new one glows.
For every dream that fades away a new one grows.
When things are not what they would seem
you must keep following your dream.
So while my heart is still believing I'll say good-bye.

Love is a sweet thing caught a moment
and held in a golden eye.
You can borrow but never own it
after a while it says good-bye.

Heavy's the heart that has to turn and say good-bye.
But as we love so do we learn, I'll say good-bye.
Cage a bird he will not sing
I can't be caged in by a ring.
So while the chilly wind is blowing I'll say good-bye.

So as the winter says hello I'll say good-bye.
I never ever did like snow I'll say good-bye.
I'm just a man and nothing more
in the face of love I'll close the door.
Because another road is calling I'll say good-bye.

for O. H.

THANK YOU

All the taxi horns have sounded their retreat.
The wind is down to nothing but a whisper in the street.
And now as you lie sleeping I'll take
a moment just to tell you
all the things I never say when you're awake.

Thank you for the raspberries this morning
and thank you for the orange marmalade.
And last night let me say
when you might have gone away
thank you very much because you stayed.

Thank you for the sun you brought this morning
even though the sky was full of clouds.
And thank you for the way
you held me yesterday
and steered me through the noisy Paris crowds.

I can't look ahead to the future
and I'm too old to run home to the past.
So now while you sleep on beside me
I'll do what I can to make this moment last.

Thank you for another special morning
and thank you for an even better day.
And thank you in advance
if there's even half a chance you'll stay,
one more morning.   One more day.

for Lee Hays

DANDELION DAYS

All our dandelion days are done
and so we'll run the fields no more
in search of wild roses
that grow out on the moor.

All our dandelion days are done
and so we'll turn our heads away
from every silver morning
and every golden day.

But sweet September's open arms
belonged to us and held us once.
Remember when the summertime
sang songs to us and only us.

All our dandelion days are done
and so we'll run the fields no more
for all the wild roses
have withered on the moor.

THE EVER-CONSTANT SEA

Once upon a time
loving set me free.
Free as any bird who ever heard
the wind blow in the trees.

After love had gone
I had merely me
and my only friend
the ever-constant sea.

We've been through it all
my old friend and me.
Summertime and fall have shown us all
the world there is to see.

So, if I love again
if love is good to me
I'll share it with my friend
the ever-constant sea.

THREE

We were three, my true friend, my new love and me.
And none were as happy as we
as we walked beside the Mediterranean Sea.

Passion grew as passion has a will and want to do
and long before the summertime was through
they walked beside the oceanside as two.

July's done. It fell beneath the knife of August sun
and long before the summertime was done
I walked beside the oceanside as one.

for Voyle Gilmore

METHINKS THOU DOTH
PROTEST TOO MUCH

Look at them little kids in their back yards
playin' with matches, burnin' draft cards.
Look at them cats called Sonny and Chér
two or three million off 'n all of that hair.
Look at them types on motorcycle bikes
roarin' through the neighborhood scarin' little tykes
hell's little angels dressed in blue
tattoos say, "Mother, I love you."
Oh the time the trials and the troubles are such
                methinks thou doth protest too much.

Look at them lily whites goin' off to church
later in the afternoon callin' John Birch.
Sendin' off letters to the P.T.A.
sayin' this teacher's red and that one's gay.
Look at them pacifists marchin' in the street
ain't nothin much worse than two left feet.
Stirrin' up rebels and racial unrest
nothin' much left to protest but protest.
Oh the times the trials and the troubles are such
                methinks thou doth protest too much.

THE LOVE CREATURE

I'm the one you often meet
between the cartoon and the feature
some have called me ugly duck
and some, the Love Creature.
Some have thought my eyes looked bright
some have thought them tired
and I couldn't count the times
my hindside's been admired.

Beauty as it's often said
lives in the mind's eye
I've been sent red roses
and once a custard pie.

I'm the one they sandwich in
between the poet and the preacher
some have called me ugly duck
and some, the Love Creature.
Sometimes false reality
obscures what I am
half of me is man all right
the other half is ham.

DO YOU KNOW ME, MARIA?

Do you know me, Maria?
I was the one in the window who smiled
I was caught in the crowd's eye
and held in your eye for a while.

Do you know me, Maria?
I was the one in the doorway who laughed
I was the one running after you
for more than a mile and a half.

And the sun went down
and the sun came up
we had spoken once in silence
that should have been enough.

Do you know me, Maria?
I was the one in the distance who cried
I was left all alone by the highway
and the highway is empty and wide.

A KIND OF LOVING

I sing songs for people I can't have
people I meet once and will never see again.
It is for me a kind of loving.
A kind of loving, for me.

I make words for people I've not met
those who will not turn to follow after me.
It is for me a kind of loving.
A kind of loving, for me.

listen to the warm

It is for love that I live all alone.
Because the lovers I imagine
are safer than the ones I've known.

I make rhymes for people who won't hear
some who will not turn their faces to meet mine.
It is for me a kind of loving.
A kind of loving, for me.

ABOUT THE AUTHOR

ROD MCKUEN was born in Oakland, California, at the end of the Depression. He grew up in California, Nevada, Washington, and Oregon, and worked as a laborer, stunt man, radio disk jockey, and newspaper columnist before serving in the army in Japan and Korea as a psychological-warfare script writer, and member of the Korean Civil Assistance Command.

Returning home he was encouraged by his friend Phyllis Diller to perform at San Francisco's Purple Onion. During the engagement he was brought to Hollywood and put under contract to Universal-International as an actor. In 1959 he moved to New York to compose and conduct the music for Albert McCleery's highly lauded television series, *The CBS Workshop.*

He has played the major cabarets and concert halls of the world, and written more than seven hundred songs. His material has been performed by Andy Williams, Danny Kaye, Elsa Lanchester, Eddy Arnold, Henry Mancini, The Kingston Trio, and Glenn Yarbrough among others. He spends seven months of the year in a house in the Hollywood hills, with a menagerie of cats and dogs, where he writes, records for RCA Victor, and runs a growing publishing and recording firm. The balance of his time he devotes to traveling and performing in Europe. This is his second volume of poetry; his first, *Stanyan Street and Other Sorrows,* was published in 1966.